Praise for *THE NOW EFFECT*
by Elisha Goldstein

What we most cherish—love, aliveness, creativity, play—arises only in moments of presence. In The Now Effect *you'll get an invaluable map for coming home to the life that is here and now. With a beautiful clarity and simplicity, Elisha Goldstein offers anecdotes, science, perennial wisdom and practical exercises that will guide you in working with difficulties and in living with an awakened heart.*

— Tara Brach, bestselling author of *Radical Acceptance*

The Now Effect *offers wise and simple guidance that is immediately helpful, compassionate and playful. It is a genuine invitation to be fully present, to open yourself up to life.*

—Jack Kornfield, bestselling author of *A Path with Heart*

The Now Effect *reminds us how to have fun with our lives again. Who would think that sitting quietly and watching our breath would teach us how to be kind, smart and have a sense of humor? With his book, Elisha Goldstein has done his part to create the conditions for world peace!*

—Chade-Meng Tan, Jolly Good Fellow
at Google and author of *Search Inside Yourself*

Elisha Goldstein, PhD, is masterful at demonstrating how moments of being aware hold space for choice, flexibility, and new perspectives. There's a freshness to the simplicity of his approach that will resonate with those new to these concepts, as well as long-term practitioners.

—Tara Healey, MEd, program director,
Mindfulness-Based Learning for Harvard Pilgrim Health Care

The Now Effect *shines with a fresh simplicity and wisdom that will make you see your mind and relationships in a different way. With practical guidance, this book gives you important tools to make changes for a better life. A genuinely uplifting and very enjoyable book.*

—Jeffrey M. Schwartz, MD, coauthor of *You Are Not Your Brain*

If you are looking for a handbook on how to improve the quality of your life, reduce your stress levels and help build a better future for yourself, your family, your community and your country, this book is it.

—Congressman Tim Ryan, author of *A Mindful Nation*

Shot through with stories, poetry, and down to earth lessons, the brief chapters in this book are entertaining but never trite and make mindfulness practice refreshingly accessible. Accompanied by Elisha's clear online video instruction, The Now Effect *will become a valuable resource for clinicians, doctors, patients, teachers, and anyone else who is looking to rediscover and rest in the present moment.*

—Pat Ogden, PhD, founder, Sensorimotor Psychotherapy Institute

These wisdom-packed offerings teach beautifully how the relevant aspects of neuroscience can help illuminate what otherwise might seem like magic: The way we pay attention to the here and now of our experience can free our minds, enhance our relationships, and transform our brains toward well-being. Soak in these powerful lessons and enjoy!

—Daniel J. Siegel, MD, author of *Mindsight: The New Science of Personal Transformation* and codirector, UCLA Mindful Awareness Research Center

Written with a lightness of touch and chock full of practical advice, this book is a broad and generous portal for those interested in bringing the power of present moment awareness more fully into their lives.
—Zindel V. Segal, coauthor of *The Mindful Way Through Depression*

Grounded in the science of how the brain tricks us to dwell in the past and the future—anywhere but now—and full of practical methods, The Now Effect *will help you feel stronger, less stressed, more present, happier, kinder, and more effective.*

—Rick Hanson, PhD, author of *Buddha's Brain:*
The Practical Neuroscience of Happiness, Love, and Wisdom

Based on ancient mind training techniques with a thoroughly modern twist, this book is a joy to read and even better to put into practice.

—Christopher K. Germer, PhD,
author of *The Mindful Path to Self-Compassion*

We all want to move beyond the dead-end, conditioned responses that derail our best intentions and hold us hostage day after day, year after year; in these pages, Elisha Goldstein offers real tools toward that end. A wonderful book!

—Sharon Salzberg, author of *Real Happiness:*
The Power of Meditation

The benefits of being in the present moment rapidly are permeating our society. The scientific evidence for its impact on improved brain function and personal happiness has been established. In this elegant, thorough approach, Dr. Goldstein offers a clear path of inspiration and practices that brings the healing and empowering effect of the Now to every aspect of our daily lives. His innovation of embedding audio-visual media in real time with written instruction offers readers an immediate ability to improve their life right Now, as they read.

—Kyra Bobinet, MD, MPH,
Aetna medical director for health and wellness innovation

ALSO BY ELISHA GOLDSTEIN

The Now Effect

Mindfulness Meditations for the Frantic Parent

Mindfulness Meditations for the Troubled Sleeper

Mindfulness Meditations *for the* Anxious Traveler

Quick Exercises to Calm Your Mind

Elisha Goldstein, PhD

ATRIA PAPERBACK

New York • London • Toronto • Sydney • New Delhi

ATRIA PAPERBACK

A Division of Simon & Schuster, Inc.
1230 Avenue of the Americas
New York, NY 10020

Copyright © 2012 by Elisha Goldstein, PhD

First Atria Paperback edition November 2012

ATRIA PAPERBACK and colophon are trademarks
of Simon & Schuster, Inc.

For information about special discounts for bulk purchases,
please contact Simon & Schuster Special Sales at
1-866-506-1949 or business@simonandschuster.com.

The Simon & Schuster Speakers Bureau can bring
authors to your live event. For more information or to
book an event contact the Simon & Schuster Speakers
Bureau at 1-866-248-3049 or visit our website at
www.simonspeakers.com.

Designed by Dana Sloan

Manufactured in the United States of America

10   9   8   7   6   5   4   3   2   1

Library of Congress Cataloging-in-Publication Data

Goldstein, Elisha.
  Mindfulness meditations for the anxious traveler / by
Elisha Goldstein.
      p.   cm.
   1. Travel—Health aspects.   2. Travel—Psychological
aspects.   3. Meditation.   4. Stress management.   I. Title.
RA783.5.G55 2012
613.6'8—dc23   2012035247

ISBN 978-1-4767-1132-4
ISBN 978-1-4516-8395-0 (ebook)

Contents

Mindfulness Meditations *for the* Anxious Traveler

Introduction

ANNE LONG ENJOYED the traveling she did for work. With all the miles she racked up, she was treated like royalty. Getting on the plane was like entering a space of free time. There were no responsibilities, and she could just relax, flip through a magazine, listen to music, or watch an entertaining movie. But a short flight from LAX to SFO on August 4, 2010, changed all of that. After experiencing extreme turbulence, she remembered hearing another passenger yell, "We're all going to die," as the person in the seat next to her grabbed her arm. Anne thought, No one's in control here. Twenty minutes later the plane made a jerky landing. Everyone was safe, but that wasn't the story Anne's mind told her.

That was only the beginning of Anne's long journey as an anxious traveler, and she's not alone. According to the VALK Foundation in the Netherlands, up to 40 percent of people experience some form of anxiety while flying. The "fear circuit" in our brain lies in a primitive area called the limbic system or emotional brain. When we're experiencing overwhelming anxiety, we don't have access to a more evolved area called the prefrontal cortex or rational brain, as fear is running the show. Anne felt that facing her anxiety about flying was the hardest thing she had ever done. She and I worked together to help her gain clarity about and mastery over her fear. The following writings and practices in this book are what we worked with, and now it's your turn to use this material to train your brain to relax, look for the good, and overcome your fear. This is the Now Effect in action.

The Space Between

In short, the Now Effect is the "Aha!" moments of clarity in life when we wake up to our truths. It's the moments when we come home after being berated by a customer and see our child running toward us that remind us of our value. It's when we hear of a friend's family member passing away and reconnect to the loved ones in our lives. It's the moment we see a baby's smile and all our stress drifts away. It was the sunny day of September 11, 2001, when many people around the world woke up and connected to what was most important. No matter how we get there, we find what is sacred and precious in life when we enter into the spaces of awareness that occur all around us.

Sometimes it seems like a cosmic joke that those spaces of clarity, which reveal the essence of life and our innate wisdom, are so slippery and so easy to become disconnected from.

The simple yet subtle truth is that life is decided in the spaces. However, the power to choose our responses comes only with an awareness of those spaces. As we practice becoming aware of the spaces in our lives, we soon come to understand that they are actually "choice points," moments in time when we are aware enough to choose a response. One response may be to bring mindfulness to whatever we're doing, including the experience of stress and anxiety that comes along with traveling, and break free from the ways of thinking and behaving that don't serve us. Mindfulness is the ability to pay attention, on purpose, while putting aside our programmed biases.

Throughout this book you'll be exposed to mindfulness practices and reflections, but you'll also turn the wheel a notch further, refining the focus with specific techniques that are tailored to prime your mind toward spaces or choice points. In a short time, those spaces of awareness will begin dropping in on you like moments of grace throughout the day, guiding you with more freedom to travel with ease.

When you think about it, there is no other time than now. Even our stories and beliefs from the past and our hopes and worries about the future are occurring right now. With mindfulness, you'll begin to notice and engage the spaces in your life and not only experience greater clarity but, throughout the process, create new experiences and stories that positively influence the way you naturally see yourself and the world. You will be changing the way you think *before* you think, realizing the Now Effect.

My Story

It was a summer night in 2001 when I found myself doing exactly what I'd sworn I would never do. There was a time in my life when I was living in San Francisco, working hard but playing *much* harder. I could often be found hanging out with friends at clubs south of Market Street, living what we called the "high life," experimenting to the point of abuse with drugs and alcohol. At the time, I was one of the top salespeople at a telecommunications company, and my mind always justified my behavior: "As long as you're doing well at work, everything is okay."

At some of the seedier clubs, there was a man I often saw who looked wasted away, as if the life had been sucked out of him, as he frantically danced all night—clearly with the support of some kind of speed. The mere sight of him would immediately make me feel disgusted. I remember turning to my friends and saying, "God help me if I ever turn out like him."

It was about 5 A.M. one Monday morning when I had been up for almost two days that I found myself in the backseat of a broken-down limousine with that very man and his equally strung-out girlfriend. She too looked like a shadow of a human being. If I'd had a mirror and my mind had been clear, I might have said the same about myself. I had intentionally sought him out at a club because I wanted to see if he had anything to help me stay awake long enough to get me through the workday. It was my darkest hour, and a voice began to percolate within me: "Please help me, how did I ever get here?" In that pain and desperation something became clear as the voice continued, "Your life is worth more than this; there are too many people who love you for you to throw it all away." In that moment I was thrust into a space of clarity where I knew what I had to do. As I jumped out of the car, I made the choice to walk all the way home and begin my recovery.

Though I'd love to tell you that in that moment I was transformed forever, that's not the way it played out, and frankly, when it comes to our deeply ingrained habits, it's not the way it plays out for most people. In the days that followed, my resolve began to weaken as I gradually stopped noticing the spaces of choice and began living on automatic again. It was just a few weeks later that I found myself engaging in the same old patterns.

The principles and practices in this book are what released me from being stuck in the habitual ways of living that didn't serve me and gave me a life of greater freedom.

The Top Benefits of the Now Effect

- You will literally change the way you think before you think and break free of subconscious beliefs and old programming that don't serve you.
- You'll have access to more choice points in life, bringing back a feeling of aliveness and opening the doors to greater potential, opportunities, and possibilities.
- You'll become more flexible in your decision making and responses to people and challenges.
- You'll increase your emotional intelligence and be able to relax more effectively in moments of distress.
- You'll open up to feeling more grateful, forgiving, loving, hopeful, empathic, and compassionate—all key components of feeling good.
- You'll tap into the wisdom that lies within you and make your intuition more reliable.
- You'll feel more connected to yourself and others, a critical ingredient of feeling well.
- You'll literally rewire a stronger and healthier brain.
- You'll change your life by breaking out of the habitual patterns of living that don't serve you.

This book is an opportunity to unlock the confines of your mind and begin a playful adventure. You will soon see the doorway into the space of awareness that might have seemed so elusive before. It's through these spaces that you will realize the Now Effect and begin to change the rest of your life.

Now take a breath, because it's time to get started.

Relax and Get Present

When I let go of what I am, I become what I might be.

—Lau Tzu

IN THE FALL of 2002 I set out on a path to figure out the most effective ways to transform stress and anxiety and live a life worth living. What I found was something that would in turn change the rest of my life. One of the fundamental facts that I came to understand through my study and practice was that in order to make any real changes in life you had to be present. Only in a state of presence can you be aware that your catastrophic thoughts aren't facts, you have tools to calm your anxious mind, and you can relax into a new reality of "what might be." Part I is dedicated to giving you the fundamentals to train your brain to be here now and will support the next two parts. You'll come to understand that you don't have to believe everything you think and will learn short practices to step out of autopilot, steady your mind, and become aware of the "choice points" all around you. You can either read and practice or link to a short video where I will guide you through it.

In the summer of 2008, Congressman Tim Ryan of Ohio was feeling the accumulation of a relentless, nonstop work schedule and was heading toward burnout. Tim was thirty-seven years old, dressing the part of a politician in conservative suits and on call at all times. He was living in two places, constantly traveling between Ohio and Washington, D.C. All the moments of his life were accounted for. He loved his work, but he knew if he didn't change something soon, it wasn't going to last. His stress level was too high, and his mind was incessantly running with stories about what he could have done better in the past and what he needed to do in the future.

He found a weeklong retreat led by Jon Kabat-Zinn called "The Power of Mindfulness," which catered to leaders in their respective fields. Tim showed up in his suit and reluctantly checked in his two BlackBerrys. About three days into the retreat he was led into thirty-six hours of silence with the purpose of practicing stepping into the space of his life as it was. Somewhere during those thirty-six hours, he told me, "I started to realize that I was not my thoughts. I had read about this in books, but for the first time I was actually experiencing a separation between my awareness and the thoughts that were running through my head. I saw the same movie playing over and over again, but I wasn't participating, just watching. As I continued to do this, for the first time in a long time my body began to relax and my head loosened up. I felt like everything was going to be okay."

There's no question that our minds are the ultimate storytellers. They tell us who we are, what we can accomplish, what's to be feared, who's to be accepted, and ultimately what we believe.

Whatever we believe powers the way we think before we think, guiding those sneaky snap judgments that make up how we see the world and our every interaction. If we believe we can't get on a plane, give a speech, lose weight, or live without our smartphones, doing those things is going to be a lot harder, if not impossible. The same goes for getting through the difficult moments in life, whether it's travel, a relationship conflict, or working through stress, anxiety, depression, or addiction.

Though no one really knows when beliefs begin to form, we do know that from the time we're in the womb we're already sensing the environment around us, taking in and processing information.

We also know that from the moment we're born our brains start to wire in what is good and bad, right and wrong, fair and unfair from our parents, religious institutions, and the media.

There's a difference between thinking and knowing that you're thinking. The latter implies having an awareness of a space between the knower (you) and the thought. The fact is, you are not your thoughts, and you don't need to be enslaved by them.

Noticing the unhealthy habitual patterns of the mind has enormous power, as it stretches the space between our awareness and the thoughts themselves. You can say, "My mind is circling that bad neighborhood again," and in that space of awareness you can redirect the energy of your mind down another road. As you practice knowing your mind, you'll begin to understand that you don't have to identify so strongly with old beliefs or unhealthy stories and can increase your sense of distance from them.

Rather than just read about the space between awareness and thoughts, let's try an exercise so you can experience it. Take a minute or so to close your eyes, get a sense of your body as it is, and imagine that you are sitting in a dark movie theater looking at the images and listening to the dialogue on the screen of your mind. While you are doing this, there's no need to create thoughts or try to change any of them; just sit back and be aware of what's there. Are there many thoughts or few? You might notice a dialogue, the thoughts we hear such as "I need to go to the grocery store," "Why am I doing this practice? I have other things to do," or "I wonder when the economy is going to pick up?" Or maybe you notice images or pictures. Check to see if you notice more dialogue or images or an equal combination of the two. As you close your eyes, see if you can notice the spaces between the thoughts themselves. Go ahead, take a few moments and give it a shot.

Watch the Movie in Your Mind
Bring attention up into your mind to notice
your thoughts, as if watching a movie.

This Now Moment gives you the experience of relating *to* your thoughts instead of *from* your thoughts. As you practice, you'll begin to recognize the space between your awareness and your thoughts, which will help you see that thoughts are simply mental events that come and go and you don't need to be enslaved by them.

1

Ask Yourself: Where Am I Starting From?

WHETHER YOU'RE EN ROUTE to the airport, halfway through the flight, or getting ready to land, three basic things are happening that make up your immediate experience: thoughts, emotions, and physical sensations. In the past many people believed the theory that the mind and body operate separately, but we now know that our experience is linked in a triangle of awareness.

Here's the triangle in action:

Triangle of Awareness

Imagine you're about to board the airplane. What do you experience first? Thoughts, emotions, or physical sensations?

As stories begin to unfold in your mind about how terrible it is going to be to ride the plane, your shoulders begin to tighten, the pit in your stomach begins to grow, and anger or fear may arise. Memories then flood in about all the past suffering you've endured on flights. As you get closer to walking into the plane, you may think, "It's going to be awful. What if there's a lot of turbulence?" The fear circuit flares up as your breath and heartbeat become more rapid and your anxiety increases. Our brains are unique, so we experience different parts of the triangle first.

This triangular drama happens rapidly, beneath your awareness. As you bring understanding and attention to the triangle, you create memories of it and alert your mind to be more aware of it. Since we know that the mind uses memories as reference points to make judgment calls and decisions, the next time you hear, "Now boarding, flight 212 to [insert your destination]," you are more likely to move out of the autopilot cycle and into a space of awareness where you can intentionally consider alternatives, practice a more flexible mind, regulate your body, and develop more reliable intuition.

Just as with reading, walking, and riding a bike, it's all about practice.

As you practice, the understanding and memory of this triangle become a reference point that your subconscious relies on to perceive the world.

One way to practice a mindful check-in is by asking yourself, "Where am I starting from right now?" This question invites your mind to mindfully check in with your body, emotions, and thoughts. I suggest practicing the mindful check-in a few times a day for the next week, at times when you're not feeling stressed, to get the hang of it. As it becomes more natural, you can start using it when the "fear circuit" comes alive. In time, you'll notice it automatically dropping in on you like moments of grace, popping you out of a stress cycle and calming your nervous system.

If you like more structure, you are welcome to experience the triangle in the following order:

1. **BODY.** Usually, underneath all the skewed stories of our minds, there is a straightforward physical feeling that arises in the body, telling us exactly what is going on. The problem is that we're trained to be up in our heads so much and are therefore cut off from our bodies that we don't realize the wisdom our bodies hold. We can use our body as a barometer to let us know what's up and as a reminder to step into the spaces in our lives.

   Take a few moments to check in with your body. Notice your posture and any sensations such as heat, coolness, achiness, tension, tightness, heaviness, lightness, pain, or looseness. Notice if your energy feels right or depleted. If you don't notice any sensation, just notice that there is no sensation; that is fine. What is your body telling you?

2. **EMOTIONS.** Go ahead and check in with your emotions. Are you frustrated, calm, happy, sad, annoyed, restless, tired, scared, or joyful? See if you can put a name to how you're feeling emotionally. Get a sense for how it feels in your body. Frustration can often feel like tension, restlessness can feel as though your body wants to move, joy can feel like expansion or looseness.

3. **THOUGHTS.** Just as we can sit back in a movie theater and watch the action on the screen, we can check in with our thoughts by being aware of what stories are being spun. They may be

thoughts about the future or the past, judgments about the mindful check-in or this book in general, or maybe nonsensical thoughts and images.

Mindful Check-in

An opportunity to give your mind
the experience of tapping into the
triangle of awareness and watering
the seeds of the Now Effect.

Whatever you find during this mindful check-in, remember that the outcome is not that important. Instead, it is an opportunity to give your mind the experience of tapping into the triangle of awareness and watering the seeds of the Now Effect. As you do this, you can start to see just how often you live on automatic and that there are more choices about how to live in this world than you realized.

2

The Narrator

JOSH WAS SITTING outside a coffee shop sipping tea when he noticed a couple next to him engaging in a PDA (public display of affection). Immediately his mind perked up: "What's wrong with them? This is ridiculous." It was impossible not to notice them, and as he did, he thought, "What's wrong with me? How come I'm not in a relationship?" Memories of his ex-girlfriend popped into his mind, and sadness about their recent breakup arose. He remembered all the good times. "Maybe I should go on one of those dating sites," he thought, "but I'll never find a match." He sank into his seat feeling more alone than ever.

When we engage with the stories in our minds at the expense of connecting with the direct experience of the present moment, we can get stuck in cycles of anxiety or depression.

The fact is, we are wired to tell stories. There's a cluster of regions in the brain that we can call the "narrative network." It goes straight up the center of the head and constantly tells stories about what we're doing, how we're doing, why something is good or bad or right or wrong, or how a problem can be fixed, or it wanders off into a daydream. We'll call this part of the brain the Narrator.

The Narrator lights up when we're in "default mode" or on autopilot. As Josh was sipping his tea, the Narrator took in the scenes, ran them through a filter, and created a story. Unfortunately, the story in Josh's mind ended with him being alone. We're trying to balance the Narrator with another key part of the brain, known as the "experiential network," which we can call the Sensor. This area lights up when we're paying attention to our senses. Research shows that the two networks are inversely correlated, meaning that when one is very active, the other is less so. So when you're sipping tea or coffee and intentionally taking in the taste, as your senses come alive, the Narrator is not as active. If your brain is on default mode or daydreaming while you're sipping, you're likely to miss out on tasting the drink.

We often perceive uncomfortable feelings as threats. The Narrator is then triggered beneath our awareness and begins to weave a story to counteract the perceived threat. But in the process it starts a cycle of rumination that unfortunately tends to dig us deeper into a feeling that something is wrong.

Identifying when the Narrator is at play creates a space between our awareness and the stories and judgments of our minds. In that space we can choose to stop interpreting the uncomfortable feeling as a threat, feel what's there, and give it space.

Next time you're feeling a strong emotion, recognize that it's likely activating the Narrator and what you need to do is activate the Sensor, which is connected to the now. You can practice a mindful check-in or say to yourself, "Breathing in, I calm my brain; breathing out, I feel my body."

3

Do a
Body Scan

ONE THING WE know about fear is it is tied to a mind trap called *catastrophizing,* playing the "what if" game around potential doom-and-gloom scenarios about flying. But those thoughts aren't facts. What is an undeniable fact is the sensation that arises in the body as constriction in the chest, shallow breathing, or tension in the shoulders. The body scan trains our minds to come down from the stories and into the body, back to the facts, interrupting the stress cycle and slowing the snowball down. The truth is, the body is a barometer for how we're feeling moment to moment, so it behooves us to develop a greater intimacy with it.

The body scan is focused on doing just that.

The following steps will guide you through preparing for the practice and then take you through a step-by-step guide to deepen your connection to the body and train your mind to realize the spaces of awareness that always exist when flying, offering you the ability to realize the Now Effect.

1. Set aside five minutes or more to sit or lie down and slowly bring awareness to sensations in your body. Move your focus progressively from your feet to your head. Sensations may include heat, coolness, tingling, itchiness, wetness, dryness, pressure, heaviness, lightness, and even pain. Use a timer or alarm to remind you when the time is up. Don't worry if you haven't made it through your whole body when the time is up. The purpose isn't to complete the whole body from head to toe but simply to practice dropping into spaces of awareness and mindfully attending to the direct experience of your body as it is right now.

2. Remember when your mind wanders off to recognize you are in a space of awareness, a "choice point" without judgment, and simply note where it has wandered to while gently guiding your attention back to your intention of being present. You can treat this as a game, starting with a short practice and slowly building up.

3. Be aware of the spaces when you move from one part of your body to the next. Recognize that in this space is a choice to intentionally guide your attention to the next part of your body.

Step-by-Step Instructions

1. **MINDFUL CHECK-IN.** Notice the position of your body. What emotions are present? What thoughts are filtering through your mind? Are there any judgments or resistance? Is your mind telling you that there are more important things to do? Whatever is there, see if you can just acknowledge it and let it be.

2. **THE BREATH AS AN ANCHOR.** Begin to gently shift your awareness to your body's breathing. Imagine that it's the first time you've ever noticed your breath. Where do you feel it? What

is the sensation like? Continue this for about a minute or until it feels right to move on.

3. **YOUR FEET AND ANKLES.** Bring your attention into your feet, and welcome any feelings that are there. As with the rest of this practice, if there are no feelings, notice what it's like to experience no feeling. Before moving up your legs, notice that you are in a space of awareness with the choice to move your attention. Now intentionally move your attention.

4. **YOUR LEGS.** Slowly guide your awareness up either one leg at a time or both legs at once. Dip your awareness into your body, feeling and allowing what is there. Notice sensations in your calves, shins, knees, and upper legs, including the hamstrings and quadriceps. Sense the density of this area of the body. Before moving on to your hips, again notice the space of awareness between stimulus and response.

5. **YOUR HIPS.** Become aware of your entire hip region. Notice and be open to any sensations in your buttocks, the sides of your hips, and your genitals. If for any reason this area of the body is triggering a response for you due to past trauma, please be sensitive to it and go at your own pace.

6. **YOUR TORSO.** You can bring your attention to your back and then move to the front or do the whole area at once. If you choose to do them separately, go up the back vertebra by vertebra and sense any feelings that arise with curiosity and without judgment. When you get to the abdominal region, breathe into your abdomen and feel it expand. Then breathe out and feel it fall. The abdomen and chest are often places where people hold emotions such as fear, love, and restlessness, among others. If you come across any emotions there, see them as simply pieces in the sandbox of your body. Name them and let them be.

7. **YOUR SHOULDERS.** This is another area that can hold tension. Being with what's here may prime your mind to be more aware of the tension you hold in your shoulders during the day, so if you notice that your shoulders are tight, it may trigger your mind into letting them relax. If your mind has been skipping over the space between one part of the body and the next, bring the awareness back now.

8. **YOUR FACE AND HEAD.** As you scan your face, be aware of any points of pressure. This is often a sign of resisting something. You can let them soften or just notice the sensations as they are.

9. **BACK TO THE BREATH.** To end the body scan, spend another minute riding the breath with your awareness with the same curiosity and sense of welcoming that you intended throughout the practice.

10. **THANK YOURSELF FOR TAKING THIS TIME.** This may seem trivial, but it sends the message internally that you care about your well-being and helps sow the seeds of resiliency.

Body Scan
Deepen your connection to your body and
train your mind to realize the Now Effect.

4

Know That Thoughts Are Not Facts

IMAGINE YOU'RE HEADING out on your trip. It's a beautiful day, and something wonderful has just happened. You're feeling good. As you're waiting for your flight, you see a friendly acquaintance. You wave and smile and the person looks at you and walks on by.

Now imagine it's a gloomy day and you have just stubbed your toe. You see the friendly acquaintance, and to the best of your ability you smile and wave, and the person just looks at you and walks on by.

Same event, different mood, and different thoughts. If thoughts were facts, they would be the same no matter what mood you're in.

The fact is that you're feeling a certain emotion, but the mental events in your mind are not facts. Wherever you're traveling, take this truth with you whenever you notice your mind circling the bad neighborhoods.

5

Stop

IN THIS MOMENT there's nowhere to go, nothing to do, except connect with your life, just as it is. Whether you're taking a plane, train, or automobile, mindfulness allows you to step into the pure awareness of your mind and body and be here for your life.

Right now, let's start by stopping. *Stop, take* a few deep breaths, and *observe* your experience. Notice how you're sitting, if there's any tension or tightness anywhere, and then allow it to soften. Observe how you're feeling emotionally, where that emotion resides in the body, and if your mind seems calm, distracted, or frenzied. There's no need to judge yourself in whatever you find. Then *proceed* by asking yourself, "As I'm traveling what would I like to pay attention to right now?" Maybe it's turning the page, talking to the person sitting next to you, or getting lost in a magazine, movie, or puzzle.

Take this moment to know that you're the captain.

6

Smile

MOST OF THE TIME our perceived worries are mistaken for facts and are inaccurate, but they take a toll on our minds and bodies.

Whether it's the night before travel or while you're on the plane, the next time you notice a worry arise, see it as a "choice point" to breathe, look at the worry, and smile at it.

See what happens.

7

Know That It's Like This

IN *THE NOW EFFECT* you'll read: "This moment, it's like this . . . and this too."

While on your journey, if the worried mind starts catastrophizing about the future, remember that every moment is just as it is, there's nothing more, and as soon as the mind goes back into the world of the past, future, memories, or dreams, you can say, "And this too."

Allow this phrase to bring you back to the present; to your life again and again.

Take this with you through this trip and into your day, dropping into what really matters.

8

Commit to a Mini-Mindful-Moment Challenge

WHETHER YOU'RE READING this before a flight, during a flight, or after a flight take this moment of awareness as an opportunity to commit to a mini-mindful-moment challenge.

Here's what you do to create the mini-mindful moment:

1. **BODY.** Notice how it is positioned, if there's any tension anywhere.
2. **EMOTIONS.** Are you angry, frustrated, calm, happy, sad, stressed?
3. **THOUGHTS.** Are you worrying, stewing, or rehashing? Are you stuck in the past or future?
4. **LOCATION.** Where are you? If you're on the plane, look out the window or at a flight map.

Just take these four steps once every hour and then breathe. You've done it!

Bring this awareness into the moments of your day outside the flight, dropping into what really matters.

9

Relax, You Are Already Home

WHEN WE ARE able to settle into truly being present to ourselves, we begin to get the sense that home lies within us. There's nothing to get because we already have it, it's all right here.

The Vietnamese Buddhist monk Thich Nhat Hanh has a wonderful phrase that helps us realize this: "Breathing in, I have arrived. Breathing out, I am home."

You can shorten it to "arrived" on the inbreath and "home" on the outbreath.

Take a minute to practice this and notice what arises.

10

Get GABA

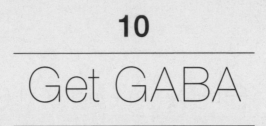

TOM WAS A client of mine who was stepping into an airport for the first time in five years after the onset of his anxiety around flying. Here's a cut from our phone call:

> **Elisha:** Can you tell me what you're feeling?
> **Tom:** I'm feeling a bit nervous.
> **Elisha:** Close your eyes for a moment; feel the connections of your feet to the floor and your body against the chair. Do you notice where you feel the fear in your body?
> **Tom:** My chest is kind of tight.
> **Elisha:** Okay, now, as you notice that feeling, say to yourself, "Fear, fear, fear."

What happened?

The amygdala, or "fear circuit," in our brain fires up when we're nervous. When we note what we're feeling we activate the prefrontal cortex or rational brain that lies behind the forehead to send out a neurotransmitter called gamma-aminobutyric acid

(GABA) to wash over this fear circuit and calm it down. GABA is our "natural Valium."

The next time you feel that fear during your travels, name what's happening and picture the front of your brain sending "natural Valium" to wash over the amygdala and cool the flames. As you practice and repeat this exercise, you can train your mind to put a space between you and your fearful experience, giving you freedom from the stress response and allowing you to gain perspective that everything is going to be okay.

11

Just Breathe

RIGHT NOW, practice:

Breathing in:

I calm my brain.

Breathing out:

I feel the gift of my body that is here.

12

Taste

ONE WAY TO come down from an anxious mind while on the move is to come to our senses. Here we have the opportunity to get in touch with taste. While airlines have become skimpier on their snacks, maybe you brought some along or purchased one in-flight. With whatever you have, pick a food or drink and dip into the magnificent gift of taste. The fact is, not everyone has this gift; there are some people who cannot taste, but you can.

Whenever your mind veers from tasting, just notice that you're thinking and gently come back to tasting.

See if you can bring a beginner's mind to this, experiencing the taste as if for the first time. What do you notice?

13

Know That Wherever You Go, Here You Are

JON KABAT-ZINN WROTE a wonderful book, *Wherever You Go, There You Are,* but perhaps it's more accurate to say, "Wherever you go, here you are."

At any given moment, whether you're waiting for a plane, sitting on the plane, or getting ready for landing, here you are.

The truth is, you're never anywhere but here.

When we learn to embrace the hereness, all things come into place.

14

Be Aware of a Single Breath

CAN YOU BE aware of a single breath? Anyone can do this.

Can you be aware of the breath coming in and going out for a single minute? This is much more difficult, but worth the playful practice. When the mind goes off, just *see* where it went, *touch* the thought, and gently *go* back to the breath, practicing *See, Touch, Go*.

As you practice this, you'll start to see some important changes taking place.

15

Realize That the Past and Future Are Now

WHEN IT COMES to being anxious, the brain is lost in fear and uncertainty about the future. The actual planning and rehearsing are happening right now, and flipping the switch from it happening on autopilot to bringing presence to it changes it entirely.

Just because there are worries about the future doesn't mean they're happening right now; in fact, it's likely they're not if you check them out. Mark Twain said, "I've had a lot of worries in my life, most of which never happened."

When you realize that the past and future are happening right now, you can learn to stop and calm the anxious mind with mindfulness, add your intelligence and heart to the moment, and cultivate an easier ride.

16

Don't Go Back
to Sleep

IN THIS MOMENT, take a few deep breaths and read these words by the thirteenth-century Persian poet and Sufi mystic Rumi:

The breeze at dawn has secrets to tell you.
Don't go back to sleep.
You must ask for what you really want.
Don't go back to sleep.
People are going back and forth across the doorsill
where the two worlds touch.
The door is round and open.
Don't go back to sleep.

Read it again on your journey, allow this moment to be the moment to wake up.

Look for the Good

Goodness is the only investment that never fails.

—Henry David Thoreau

IMAGINE THAT YOU are getting ready to head out to the airport and in your inbox you see five emails. Four of them greet you with some form of salutation and a good wish such as "Hey, how are you doing, hope your trip is great." The fifth reads, "You're a jerk, and I hope this is an awful trip." Which one sticks out in your mind? If you're like most people, the negative comment seems to be stickier. In fact, if I were to hook up your brain to a brain-imaging machine, we would see a greater surge of electrical activity in your brain connected to the negative comment. The fact is, the brain is more sensitive to unpleasant events than to pleasant ones.

Our brains are built this way to keep us out of danger. If we walk up a path and come to a fork in the road, one road leading off that has bear tracks on it and one that doesn't, our brains automatically shift our attention to the bear tracks and send us a warning not to take that route.

Without an awareness of this negativity bias, we can allow it to seep into the way we see travel, creating anticipatory anxiety, panic, and even depression. However, with awareness, we can begin to see the spaces where we get hooked into this bias, step outside of them, and gain a wiser perspective.

To influence and balance out this subconscious negativity bias while traveling, we need to actively incline our minds toward the good. I'm not advocating that you wear rose-colored glasses; this is all based on research out of places like Harvard, Stanford, the University of Wisconsin, UCLA, and more. Studies show that the more we're able to train our mind toward states of kindness, compassion, hope, gratitude, love, altruism, forgiveness, and meaning, the more we neutralize difficult emotions and are resilient in the face of difficulty. In this section you'll find practical exercises and reflections that will prime your mind toward the good, building a stronger and better brain.

17

Prime Your Mind for Good

JOHN CACIOPPO IS a psychologist and researcher at the University of Chicago who conducted a study showing how our brains become more activated when presented with negative stimuli versus positive stimuli. This research showed us the neuroscience behind the theory that our brains are biased toward the negative.

Our brains are constantly on the lookout for danger, so of course they're biased. However, when it comes to flying, it's not that helpful for the brain to be caught in a cycle of fear, revving up our nervous system, tensing our bodies, and making the flight unbearable.

It's important to practice priming the mind for good to create balance.

Say this to yourself right now: Unexpected good is on its way to me; all I have to do is be open to receive this newfound goodness. Be on the lookout for it; it may already be here.

18

Practice Freedom

BASICALLY, LEARNING THEORY teaches us that what we practice and repeat in life becomes automatic. Neuroscience has backed that up with recent studies showing how we can change our brain architecture by intentionally paying attention in particular ways.

So wherever you are on your trek, see this as a "choice point" from which to practice freedom right now.

1. Reflect upon certain styles of thinking or behaving that are connected to anxiety while traveling. Recognize them in the moment that they're occurring. Call the thought out (e.g., catastrophic thinking, overeating, grumpiness, etc.).
2. Recognize how this moment feels in the body. This will ground you to the reality of the moment.
3. Release the feeling by saying, "Breathing in, I acknowledge the feeling that's here; breathing out, I release it."
4. Redirect your attention to something that is healthier and/or more important to pay attention to.

Continue this for the entire trip or as long as it feels right to you.

19

Practice Loving Everyone

LOVING-KINDNESS PRACTICE HAS been called the healer of fear. Though many know this process as *metta* practice from Buddhist philosophy, the practice of loving-kindness has been found among many peoples, including the Greeks, who called it *agape;* Jews, who practiced *chesed;* and Christians, who practiced centering prayer. Getting in touch with our hearts is something that millions of people have found helpful when cultivating more kindness toward themselves, their fellow travelers, their community, and the world.

In this practice we are cultivating wishes or aspirations, starting with someone we care about. Then we move on to ourselves, then to someone who is neutral, then to someone whom we are having difficulty with, and then to all our fellow travelers, our community, and the world. This is not an affirmation practice; we are not telling ourselves something that is not there at the moment, we are simply wishing ourselves and others to be happy, healthy, free from harm, and free from fear. You can come up with your own wishes for yourself, but they should be things you can also wish for others.

The following are some examples of phrases you can use for yourself and others during this practice:

May I be safe and protected from inner and outer harm.
May I be truly happy and deeply peaceful.
May I live my life with ease.
May I have love and compassion for myself.
May I love myself completely, just the way I am.
May I be free from fear.

Play around with this, and allow your experience to be your best teacher.

Loving-kindness
Wish yourself and others to be happy,
healthy, safe, and free from fear.

20

Appreciate Miracles

BEING IN OR OUT of an airplane is an opportunity to witness the miracles of life. Look outside and witness the shapes of clouds, rays of sunshine, or raindrops if they're there. Behold the colors and shapes. Listen and notice if you hear the laughter of joy or the cry of a young baby. You might consider it a miracle that you have the gift of sight or hearing. Just as the clouds cover the sun but the sunshine is always there, when we're stuck in stress and anxiety we don't notice these miracles of life, but as we drop into awareness we realize they're always there.

21

Count Your Blessings

THE GIFT OF LIFE, the beauty of nature, a smile or hug from a loved one, or attention from someone can bring on a feeling of gratitude. However, when we're not feeling 100 percent, the mind misses this essential component of being alive and a wonderful source of resiliency in the face of what's difficult.

Put all your judgments aside, and contemplate five things you are grateful for right now. Don't just automatically list them; bring some mindfulness to each one, being aware of the gratitude and noticing how it feels in your body and mind.

22

Look Around for the Good

TAKE THIS MOMENT to look around. Where is the good in this moment? Look inside and out. What's good within you, what's good outside of you?

The gifts of life are truly here; we just need to come to our senses from time to time to notice them.

23

Build Self-Trust

As we learn to drop down from the busyness in our minds and into the now, we can cultivate self-trust and self-reliance.

—The Now Effect

SET THE INTENTION to be on the lookout for moments that your mind seems busy, anxious, distracted, or cluttered. Ask yourself, "Are these thoughts true?" Then ask, "What am I feeling right now?" Practice bringing a curious and friendly awareness to the sensation. Little by little we start to recognize that we can "be with" ourselves even in difficult mind states and that "It's going to be okay," building a sense of self-trust, self-reliance, and opening up to what really matters.

24

Plant the Seeds of Today

THERE IS A well-known proverb, "All the flowers of all the tomorrows are in the seeds of today."

Do yourself a favor: read that quote again, and allow your mind to see it as if for the very first time.

Ask yourself, "When was the last time I actually intentionally paid attention to the seeds I plant day by day or moment to moment?"

While you're traveling is a perfect time to ask yourself if you're planting seeds of negative thinking, self-judgment, catastrophic thinking, or isolation. Or are you planting seeds of gratitude, laughter, giving, and compassion?

This isn't meant to be Pollyannaish; it's just a very practical way to influence how our minds work.

Basically, what we practice, we receive. So what are you practicing at home, at work, with friends, and even on vacation? It's worth taking an inventory.

Some people wait their whole lives before realizing the seeds they've planted. You can do so now.

Visualize this. Let it guide you in this moment as you plant the seeds of your garden.

25

Be an Ambassador of Compassion

WHEN SITTING ON a plane, see the "choice point" by considering all the other people on the plane who are also struggling with being an anxious traveler. Remember, up to 40 percent of people struggle with some form of anxiety about traveling. Be an ambassador of compassion, connecting with your heart and saying:

May you feel safe and protected.
May you be at ease.
May you be free from this fear.
May you be happy.

26

Don't Underestimate Your Power

DOUBTING IS A mind trap that can be a major hindrance. A new situation is presented, and your mind doubts that you can handle it. This then becomes a self-fulfilling prophecy as the mind looks for evidence to reinforce that belief.

Look back into your past, and you'll find moments of insight, mindfulness, acceptance, and compassion.

A simple practice such as putting your hand on your heart and doing a mindful check-in, being the ambassador of compassion, or just breathing allows you tap into a space of awareness and water the seeds of choice, power, growth, and freedom that have always been inside you.

27

Know That Everyone Wins

WHEN YOU CULTIVATE the power of mindfulness, you begin to experience more peace, happiness, and joy. This kind of presence is attractive and encourages the light in others to come out. Everybody wins.

In this space of awareness, settle into the very is-ness of this moment, cultivating presence. Close your eyes and imagine your awareness is as vast as the sky all around you. Allow the various phenomena to appear within this vast awareness. Sounds are just mental events arising and falling away, leaving no trace. Sensations shift and change while thoughts appear and disappear. You just sitting in this seat of mindfulness are open, balanced, spacious, and untouchable. Everything is okay.

28

Be Mindful of Your Diet

TODAY IS A day to be mindful of your diet, not just the food you take in but what you take into all your senses—eyes, ears, nose, mouth, and sense of touch. Traveling gives you ample opportunity to ask:

What kind of diet are you feeding your senses?

Are you spending too much time with the news? Are your senses on sensory overload from too much interaction with digital devices?

What good things might you bring into your diet? Is there music you'd like to listen to? The touch of a loved one? A specific food? Maybe you're at a terminal that has a beautiful landscape, or if you're in flight, there's the wonder of clouds or mountains just outside.

Allow today to be the day, in this Now Moment, to start feeding a life of meaning.

29

Look for Hidden Treasure

REMEMBER, AS VIKTOR Frankl said: "Between stimulus and response there's a space. In that space lies our power to choose our response. In our response lies our growth and our freedom."

Where are the spaces in your life, the "choice points," where you can choose to respond differently?

Be on the lookout for them today and find the choices, possibilities, and wonder in everyday moments.

Allow this to be playful, like a child on a treasure hunt.

30

Be a Loving Being

AT THE CORE you are a loving being; we all are. But in order to access that love, which can be so healing of the difficulties in life, you must be present. The truth is, we can all do this and be here for our lives; it's a practice that starts right now.

If all you did was put your hand on your heart and wish yourself well, it would be a moment well spent. Bring this loving intention to other people in your life.

31

Think About Your Memorable Moments

CLOSE YOUR EYES and think of a recent good experience, something that brings up feelings of joy, laughter, love, or maybe great peace. Allow yourself to really imagine the scenario: what was happening, who was there, and where you were.

Pause the scene at its peak, giving yourself this gift, noticing how it feels in the body, savoring it, and priming your mind for good.

32

Listen to the Life Within

ONE OF THE greatest gifts—and hindrances—of our minds is to automatize things in life after practicing and repeating them many times. Walking without having to consider every step makes things a lot easier.

However, one of the greatest habits of the mind is to constantly look outside ourselves for clarity.

There's a lot we can get from reading blogs, books, and interviews and listening to other commentators, but at the end of the day the greatest teacher is ourselves, our own experience.

Confucius said: "I am thinking of giving up speech."

Zigong said: "If you did not speak, what would there be for us, your disciples, to transmit?"

The Master said: "What does Heaven ever say? Yet there are the four seasons going round and there are the hundred things coming into being. What does Heaven ever say?"

—*Analects* XVII

(from *Confucius from the Heart* by Yu Dan)

But how can we ever listen to the clarity and wisdom of our experience if we never stop to do so?

Take a moment now to do a mindful check-in (please see page 14). Ask yourself, "What do I need right now?" Give yourself the gift of listening to the life within.

Transform
Your Fear

Love is what we were born with. Fear is what we learned here.

—Marianne Williamson

THE **THIRTEENTH-CENTURY SUFI** poet Rumi wrote, "This being human is a guest-house. Every morning a new arrival, a joy, a depression, a meanness. . . . Welcome and entertain them all!" You may think, "Welcome and entertain them all? Are you crazy? Why would I want to welcome and entertain those horribly uncomfortable feelings that come along with traveling? All I want to do is get away from them, far, far away!" Some of us avoid traveling entirely, others self-medicate with drugs and alcohol, still others just grit their teeth and get through it.

The only problem is that the uncomfortable emotions have nowhere to go; they're still within us. We cannot push them away, because they are unable to leave our minds. In pushing and struggling with them, we treat them like enemies and give energy to the distress. Rumi continued in his poem, "Still, treat each guest honorably. He may be clearing you out for some new delight." The truth is, the difficult moments that accompany our travels can actually be our greatest teachers and sources of growth.

Your work up to this point has been in service of giving you the tools and ability to relate to your difficulties in a radically different way. You can now see the space between stimulus and response that holds the "choice points," and you have the tools to widen that space, prime your mind for good, and bolster your resiliency during difficult moments.

Part III is going to take you one step further and give you the tools to radically shift your relationship to the difficult emotions that arise while traveling. As you enter into the following pages, you'll see that you can befriend your fear instead of running from it, get past your past, turn your frustrations with traveling into something constructive, and find joy and wisdom within your troubles.

What you may have thought was your enemy can now become your teacher.

33

Welcome Your Pain

WHEN I WAS six years old, my parents brought me and my two sisters into the living room, and before I had any clue what was going on, both of my sisters burst into tears. My parents proceeded to tell us that they were getting a divorce and from now on we would be living in two separate places. I stood there blankly. Concerned by my stoic reaction, my mom came up to me and asked, "What's wrong, Elisha, do you know what's going on?" To which I angrily replied, "Yeah, I know, what do you want me to do, bang my head against the wall so I'll cry?" I hadn't a clue what to do with the anger and confusion inside me, so I expressed it with willfulness.

At that time we didn't have much money, but we would occasionally go out to dinner. Even as a six-year-old, I didn't think we should be going out to dinner, and often the way I dealt with my anger was by hiding under the table and refusing to eat. My anger was not about the money but about my perception that it was wrong and unfair that our family had been torn apart. Now that I have my own kids, I look back on that time and have a lot of empathy for my parents. What do you do with a six-year-old who refuses to eat and hides defiantly under the table?

Years later, my wife noticed that whenever I got angry, I would shut down emotionally and get busy cleaning the house, washing the dishes, or checking out on the computer. If I was sitting with her, often my mind would go blank and my body would go numb. One day when I was in therapy the same thing occurred, and my therapist asked, "Elisha, where are you? It's like you're still hiding under the table." That phrase dropped me into a space of clarity. She was absolutely right. I saw that little boy inside, frightened and angry, feeling unsafe. I was freed by the realization because I was no longer controlled by my typical reaction to anger. There was now a space between me and the little boy, and in that space my heart softened. I felt a sense of compassion for my child self, and in that space I let him know that I was here and it was all going to be okay. I notice such spaces a lot more now, and often in the same moment that anger is triggered, compassion seems to gracefully arise. This is the Now Effect at work.

Ask yourself how you hide under the table. Write down a list of whatever comes to mind. Is it uncomfortable to engage in certain relationships? Do you avoid certain trips because they arouse fear? What would it be like to use the emotion as a reminder that you have entered into a choice point and experiment with Rumi's words of welcoming joys and sorrows?

As a difficulty arises, check where it is in your body and you can say, "Breathing in, I feel the fear; breathing out, I welcome what's here."

Check in right now to notice if seeing emotions as a support to bring you into the present moment brings up any physical or emotional discomfort. Make a mental note to practice welcoming what is there and relating to it with kindness. As you do so, you are present in a space of awareness, cultivating a trust that everything will be okay and opening the door for the gifts to reveal themselves.

Welcome Meditation

Check in to notice if seeing emotions as a support to bring you into the present moment brings up any physical or emotional discomfort; make a mental note to practice welcoming what is there and relating to it with kindness.

34

You Are Not a Slave

A FEW YEARS ago, I was at the local playground, watching my son jumping off a step that was about six inches high. Each time he would get up on the step with glee, take a few moments to adjust his feet, and then jump with a huge smile and break out in laughter, clearly having the time of his life. It was amazing how much fun he could squeeze out of such a simple action. It made me wonder why adults lose sight of the joy in small things.

As it turns out, our brains are wired to "enslave" our present experiences and even our future anticipations with our past experiences so that we miss out on the uniqueness of what's happening in the now.

This is called top-down processing. By engaging in bottom-up processing, we can turn a flight into a playful practice. The next time you're traveling, be curious about one thing you encounter. It could be the sip of a drink, the sound of a baby laughing, the sight of clouds, the touch of the air, or simply awareness of your physical sensations, emotions, or thoughts. As soon as you notice your mind wandering off, you are in a space of awareness; gently bring your attention back to your intention. Come back to bottom-up processing, and tune in to the direct experience of the present moment.

35

Just a Sensation

THE FACT IS, emotions are expressed through our bodies. Fear and anxiety are often felt as some form of tightening, a rapid heartbeat, shallow breathing, or maybe a clenching of the jaw. When we see the emotion just as it is, a sensation expressed in the body, it loses its power over us.

When you experience uncomfortable emotions standing in the line of the terminal, on the airplane, or anywhere else, try seeing what happens when you recognize it as "just a sensation."

Take this phrase with you, and allow your experience to be your guide.

36

An Unlikely Teacher

What you may have thought was your enemy can now become your teacher.

—*The Now Effect*

IT'S NOT THE difficulties in life that make us miserable, It's how we relate to them. If a difficult moment arises in relationship to flying, put your hand on your heart, recognizing the difficulty of the moment and sensing the power of self-compassion.

37

A Wise Phrase

It is what it is, while it is.
—The Now Effect

NOTHING LASTS FOREVER. Difficulties will pass and so will the wonders; tune in to the preciousness of life.

Bring this awareness into the moments of your day, tuning in to what really matters.

38

Freedom from Fear

DROPPING INTO PRESENCE is like dropping down into the depths of the ocean. On the surface of the ocean are waves, sometimes calm, other times lashing together in response to the weather on the surface. The fear that arises while traveling is simply a wave on the ocean.

In your mind, drop down to the depths of the ocean, look up at the wave of fear, and you will see its impermanence as clear as day. The wave may thrash around, but your awareness is not affected. You are safe, grounded, present, and free from fear.

39

Embracing What's Difficult with Love

DIFFICULTIES THAT ARISE do not go away when battled. Don't fight against fear or self-judgments. Turn toward them with a tender heart, as if they were a young baby in fear or pain. Know that a difficult feeling is a piece of you that wants to be cared for: if you treat it with neglect or abuse it will lash out; if you tend to it with love and embracing, it will feel comforted.

40

Getting Past
Your Past

WHICHEVER EXPERIENCES IN life have led up to the feelings of anxiety about flying, know that fear is yesterday. It's the habit of the mind to look for the emotionally charged memories and use them to anticipate the future. This is a waste of our attention because it takes us into old traumas and away from being present to this life.

It's important that when you notice this occurring, you have ways to deal with it, training your mind to be present to what matters.

When you notice this old suffering creeping in, say to yourself, "Breathing in, seeing the old story here; breathing out, releasing this story and stepping back into this present moment."

As you continue to do this, you will begin to see that living with greater ease is possible, allowing the Now Effect to take root.

41

We Are Not Islands

The fact is, we are not islands, and we are far more connected than we know.

—The Now Effect

TAKE A MOMENT to look around you and see who is there. All of those people are just like you, with the same deep desire to belong, to be accepted, to be loved.

As you read these words you sit in a "choice point." Choose to picture all of them in your mind right now, sensing into your connection and saying, "Just like me."

FACES CONFERENCES
4510 N FLECHA DR
TUCSON, AZ 857186726

03/28/2014   10:46:33
Merchant ID: 000000001523495
Terminal ID: 01282332
227467583992

CREDIT CARD

VISA SALE

CARD #   XXXXXXXXXXXX8367
INVOICE   0005
Batch #:   00066
Approval Code: 03461
Entry Method: Swiped
Mode: Online

SALE AMOUNT $7.50

42

You Can Always Begin Again

WHEN WE STRAY from our intentions, whether bringing mindfulness to experience or trying to be more forgiving and compassionate with ourselves, thoughts of failure can rain down: "Great, I'm back at square one."

The beauty of mindfulness is that it teaches us that no matter what the problem is, it can be worked with.

We can always begin again!

Let this knowledge support you in the moments of your day.

43

Being With

THE THIRTEENTH-CENTURY PERSIAN poet Rumi said: "Don't turn away. Keep your gaze on the bandaged place. That's where the light enters you."

Here is yet another quote that points to the reality of what most of us habitually try to avoid or react to.

The way to emotional freedom as an anxious traveler or in everyday life is through "being with" and embracing that which is painful or difficult in us rather than "trying to fix," push away, or run from it.

This is the path toward the Now Effect.

If you notice emotional discomfort arising, try putting your hand on your heart or abdomen and saying, "Breathing in, I feel you; breathing out, I am here with you."

44

One Step at a Time

SAM WAS A client who had a major fear of flying. I spent time on the phone with him as he arrived at the airport, went through security, and was about to get on the plane. He engaged the process mindfully and felt at ease up until the point when boarding began. Fear seized his body as he hunkered down to the airport seat white-knuckling the arms of the chair.

Elisha: What's happening now?

Sam: I can't do it, I can't fly.

Elisha: Do you notice how your body feels?

Sam: Constricted in my chest, breathing rapidly.

Elisha: Put your hand on your belly, and take a few deep breaths.

Sam: Okay, that feels a little better, but I still can't fly.

Elisha: You don't need to fly, can you stand?

Sam: Yes.

Elisha: Can you walk toward the line? Just the line, nothing else.

Sam (hesitantly): Yes, I think so.

Elisha: Great, let's just do one thing at a time. What's happening now?

Sam: Because I'm feeling scared, my shoulders are tight.

Elisha: As you walk, bring attention to the shoulders, roll them, and give them a mental rub.

Sam: The woman is asking for my ticket.

Elisha: Okay, just think about handing her your ticket, nothing else.

Sam: I did it!

Sam made it onto the flight that day with a powerful lesson in hand. When the mind pictures the mountain you're about to climb, focus on one step at a time, and before you know it, you'll be there.

45

Make Peace with Your Imperfections

THE JAPANESE ZEN Buddhist Dogen Zenji said, "To be in harmony with the wholeness of things is not to have anxiety over imperfections." The news flash is that we are *all* imperfect, and that is okay. Accepting ourselves as imperfect doesn't mean that you should become complacent and not make plans or not take action to gain freedom over the anxiety around traveling. It simply means operating from the perspective that we are all imperfect, so we can begin practicing kindness, instead of fear and hate, toward our imperfections when they arise.

Is there a part of you that believes that something is wrong with you or are you ashamed because you have been an anxious traveler? Isn't it time to make peace with your imperfections, cultivate compassion, and realize greater emotional freedom?

Practice "Breathing in, I open myself to what's vulnerable; breathing out, I let go of the need to be perfect."

46

The Good Side
of Anger

THE REALITY IS, it can be downright frustrating to constantly be gripped by some form of fear while traveling. At times we might even find ourselves taking our anger out on others. Maybe the unknowing victim is a friend, the guy who's taking our armrest, or the airline attendant who doesn't seem to be fast enough. But maybe there's some good that can come from our anger.

Anger or frustration provides energy that can help you break through barriers. At times the energy of that frustration is exactly what you need to give you strength to meet the fear and stand in an energy of presence, recognizing that you are not your fear, you are so much more.

47

Give Up Hope for a Better Past

IN *THE NOW EFFECT* I quoted Lily Tomlin as saying, "Forgiveness means giving up all hope for a better past." At times we can be hard on ourselves about the time gone by of struggling, flying, or other aspects of life. Take this moment to recognize that the past is the past; there's nothing about it that can be changed.

This moment right now is a fresh moment, a choice point to practice, "Breathing in, I acknowledge this painful past; breathing out, I forgive myself and release the burden from my heart and mind."

Practice this for as long as it is supportive to you.

48

The Nature of You

THERE'S A FUNNY cartoon of a woman sitting in meditation practice that reads, "I want to live in the present moment, unless that moment is unpleasant, and then I'd rather eat a cookie." If our mind is making up stories about how awful the flight is going to be, of course we're going to experience resistance to being on the plane; it's the nature of our brains to want to avoid what's unpleasant and move toward what's pleasant.

However, the moment we accept the nature of our mind, we are present in a "choice point" to begin to see through the difficult and into the good that might be there.

The good comes in the form of self-compassion, acceptance, happiness, and freedom.

49

Your ACE
in the Hole

ACE IS AN ACRONYM that I taught Anne to break out of autopilot, steady her mind, deepen her connection to this moment, and begin a process of befriending her difficult feelings.

A: **Awareness** of your thoughts, feelings, and sensations. For example, you may notice worried thoughts about an upcoming vacation and be feeling anxious. This feeling is expressed in your body as a rapid heartbeat or a constriction in the chest. Or maybe there is looseness and a sense of calmness and your thoughts are moving more slowly. The purpose of awareness is to break out of autopilot and come into the now.

C: **Collecting** your attention to your breath. In this practice we're not simply taking a few deep breaths; instead, we're allowing our attention to rest easily on the natural rhythms of the breath. You might choose to see where you notice the breath most prominently. Is it at the tip of the nose, in the chest, or in the stomach? During this practice your mind will wander to all its stories, and that is perfectly fine. Play with your attention, knowing that there's no need to judge the wandering mind. Instead you can bring curiosity to where it wandered and in that space of awareness choose a different response—to gently bring your mind and attention back to the breath.

E: **Expanding** your attention throughout your entire body. This is different from naming how your body is feeling. It is training your mind to be with what is happening now and is another way to accept the reality of what is here and letting it be. Sadness may be expressed as heaviness in the face or chest; anger may be seen in a tightening of your muscles, fear may be felt in a rapid heartbeat. Bring a beginner's mind to the feeling, along with kind attention.

Start off by practicing ACE for just a few minutes right now. After the practice, reflect on what you noticed during the space you created. What's most important to pay attention to right now? Maybe it's making a phone call to a friend or family member you've been putting off. If you are not experiencing a difficulty at the moment, you can still give this practice a try. Just engaging in the practice plants a seed in your memory, making it more likely to be recalled when you're preparing to fly.

Break Out of Autopilot
Steady your mind, deepen your
connection to this moment, and
befriend whatever difficulty is there.

The Anxious Traveler Lessons

THESE PRACTICES AND reflections were enormously helpful for getting rid of Anne's worries, cultivating her self-compassion, and expanding her space of awareness to choose how she wanted to approach the situation. Recognizing the impermanence of the feeling allowed her to feel safer about becoming curious about her fear. As she did so, she transformed from feeling out of control of her fear to feeling in control of her fear.

Once you've calmed down the emotional brain, you can engage the rational brain and remind yourself of the fact that far more people are killed in car accidents every year than in plane crashes. Or that you have a greater chance at being killed by a bolt of lightning than being in a plane crash.

Learning how to come down from the catastrophes in your mind helps you see that you don't need to believe everything you think. In the "choice points," you have skillful ways, that are portable, of coming down from your busy mind and connecting to the reality of the present moment. Inevitably this sends the message internally that "everything is going to be okay."

Be kind to yourself. It may not be an easy process, but it's important for you to be easy on yourself. It's too easy to get down on yourself when anxiety continues to creep in, but soon we see that fear can be an unlikely teacher into a wiser perspective.

Be kind to others. Whenever we're feeling imbalanced, the people around us can easily push our buttons. Plato said, "Be kind, for everyone you meet is fighting some battle." When you notice irritation with others arising, see if you can practice wishing them well, to be free from fear and at ease. This can transform your negative energy into something more supportive.

This was the exact message that Anne realized, and with guidance and practice, you can realize it too. Taking time out of your daily busyness to engage in these reflections and practices is an enormous act of self-care. The reality is, engaging the spaces of your life can take a lot of courage, especially when what's present in that space is fear.

Practice these exercises before or while you travel. Each time you do these practices, congratulate yourself for taking this time to live the Now Effect.

When you're ready to go deeper, you can graduate to the full text of *The Now Effect: How This Moment Can Change the Rest of Your Life,* to get a fuller understanding of how the Now Effect can go beyond your anxiety about flying to transform all aspects of your life.

Now bring this into your day and into your travels.

Notes

Chapter 1: Ask Yourself: Where Am I Starting From?

The term *mindful check-in* was first coined by my friend, colleague, and mentor Bob Stahl, PhD. It was included in Bob Stahl and Elisha Goldstein, *A Mindfulness-Based Stress Reduction Workbook* (Oakland: New Harbinger, 2010). I have since adapted it for *The Now Effect.*

Chapter 2: The Narrator

In 2007, Norman A. S. Farb, Zindel V. Segal, Helen Mayberg, Jim Bean, Deborah McKeon, Zainab Fatima, and Adam K. Anderson published the study "Attending to the Present: Mindfulness Meditation Reveals Distinct Neural Modes of Self-Reference," *Social Cognitive and Affective Neuroscience* 2, no. 4: 313–22. This study showed us where the story of *me* resides in our brains.

In 2010, Farb and his colleagues conducted a follow-up study, "Minding One's Emotions: Mindfulness Training Alters the Neural Expression of Sadness," *Emotion* 10, no. 1: 25–33, showing that activating the experiential area of the brain is what regular mindfulness practitioners do when exposed to sad scenes, rather than engaging with the narrative area, which can lead to rumination and inevitably depression.

Chapter 7: Know That It's Like This

Ajahn Chah was a Thai meditation master who used to say, *"Ben yung nee"* ("It's like this"). I have had many students, teachers, friends, and colleagues who have benefited from bringing this simple phrase into their life.

Chapter 16: Don't Go Back to Sleep

Coleman Barks is the most widely read translator of the thirteenth-century Sufi poet Rumi. He has translated one of the Rumi books, *The Essential Rumi: Jalal al-Din Rumi* (San Francisco: HarperSanFrancisco, 1995), among many others.

Look for the Good

Tiffany A. Ito, Jeff T. Larsen, N. Kyle Smith, and John T. Cacioppo conducted the study "Negative Information Weighs More Heavily on the Brain: The Negativity Bias in Evaluative Categorizations," *Journal of Personality and Social Psychology* 75, no. 4 (1998): 887–900, in which they showed thirty-three participants pictures meant to arouse positive feelings, neutral feelings, and negative feelings. Though the positive and negative feelings both activated greater activity in the brain, the negative pictures aroused the most of all.

For the connection of resiliency to mindfulness, Richard J. Davidson, Jon Kabat-Zinn, Jessica Schumacher, Melissa Rosenkranz, Daniel Muller, Saki F. Santorelli, Ferris Urbanowski, Anne Harrington, Katherine Bonus, and John F. Sheridan worked together to produce the groundbreaking study "Alterations in Brain and Immune Function Produced by Mindfulness Meditation," *Psychosomatic Medicine* 65, no. 4 (2003): 564–70. Since this time there has been an exponential amount of research in the field of mindfulness and neuroscience.

Chapter 21: Count Your Blessings

Robert A. Emmons and Michael E. McCullough are psychologists who conducted a research study, "Counting Blessings Versus Burdens: An Experimental Investigation of Gratitude and Subjective Well-Being in Daily Life," *Journal of Personality and Social Psychology* 84, no. 2 (2003): 377–89, that found that over the course of ten weeks, those who counted their blessings scored higher on well-being scales than those who counted burdens or neutral events.

Chapter 25: Be an Ambassador of Compassion
I'm deeply indebted to all the clients I work with and here is a term that arose within treatment.

Chapter 34: You Are Not a Slave
In 2001, Andreas K. Engel, Pascal Fries, and Wolf Singer published "Dynamic Predictions: Oscillations and Synchrony in Top-Down Processing," *Nature Reviews Neuroscience* 2, no. 10: 704–16, using the word "enslave" to describe how top-down processing can control our perception.

Chapter 41: We Are Not Islands
The phrase "Just like me" originated from Stanford psychologist and neuroscientist Philippe Goldin, PhD.

Chapter 46: The Good Side of Anger
In 1995, Daniel Goleman first published his influential book *Emotional Intelligence* (New York: Bantam), challenging people to understand the importance of attuning to their emotions in everyday life. Since then, there has been an exponential rise in exploring emotional intelligence in psychology, business, sports, and politics, among other disciplines. In 2003, Goleman published *Destructive Emotions: How Can We Overcome Them? A Scientific Dialogue with the Dalai Lama* (New York: Bantam), which helps us understand new ways of relating to our difficult emotions.

About the Author

ELISHA GOLDSTEIN, PHD, has a private practice in West Los Angeles. He is the author of *The Now Effect* and coauthor of *A Mindfulness-Based Stress Reduction Workbook* and author of the *Mindful Solutions* program series. He is the founder of the *Mindfulness and Psychotherapy* column on psychcentral.com and a frequent contributor to the *Huffington Post*. He lives in Santa Monica, California.